Expect The Unexpected While Overcoming Your Greatest Fears

Defeat Self-Doubt, Eliminate Worry, Build Positive Relationships and Learn Healthy Habits

By Kurt Reece-Peeplez

I0134026

Expect The Unexpected While Overcoming Your Greatest Fears

Expect The Unexpected While Overcoming Your Greatest Fears

Defeat Self-Doubt, Eliminate Worry, Build Positive Relationships and Learn Healthy Habits

By Kurt Reece-Peeplez

The Solz Group Publishing

Phoenix, AZ U.S.A.

kurtrp@thesolzgroup.com
kurtrp@kurtrp.com

thesolzgroup.com
kurtrp.com

Published by:
The Solz Group Publishing
Phoenix, AZ U.S.A.

thesolzgroup.com
kurtrp.com

ISBN Paperback: 978-1-63795-916-9

Printed in the United States of America

Table of Contents

About the Author

Kurt Reece-Peeplez is the Founder and President of The Solz Group which helps business owners overcome obstacles and reach new heights of personal and professional growth. He is a business coach, youth sports coach, and entrepreneur who looks to be a blessing to everyone around him.

kurtrp@kurtrp.com

kurtrp.com

Foreword

Any fear can be overcome. First, you have to examine your fears and not just ride the emotion. Upon further review, you'll find that most if not all of your fears are manageable and you will be able to negotiate the outcomes.

I've faced many fears in my life and have found through my own experience and of those around me that we have nothing to be afraid of at all. When you apply knowledge and understanding to your circumstance fear becomes an option. I'll show you how to do this so you can choose to make life better.

Enjoy this book and live your life full of options and free of fear. I wrote this especially for you.

The G.O.A.T

"The greatest fear of all time is the current fear you have for which there is no apparent solution or answer. Or is it?"

The term G.O.A.T. or Greatest of All Time is a term used mostly about great athletes in their respective sports. These athletes are almost always champions, have consistently beaten the odds, and are consistently a winner.

There is a group of great athletes in every sport, but who is the greatest of the great? Who is the greatest of all time in basketball, football, or baseball? Who is the greatest coach of all time? What is the greatest play of all time?

The debate goes on and on because there is no consensus greatest of all time that everyone agrees upon. The vote will always be split between 3-5 players, coaches, or plays.

There is a disparity in the answers because the opinions are based on individual perspectives, experience, and knowledge.

Fear is no different. If you were to ask 100 people what the greatest fear of all time is, you would get several answers. The answers are based on perspective, personal experience, and knowledge. Everyone has a different life experience so everyone will not have the same fears.

If you have a good-paying job and money in the bank, you have no fear of your cell phone being turned off for lack of payment. You may choose not to pay it, but there is no fear that you cannot pay it. If you don't have enough money to pay the bill, and don't have a way to get the rest of the money to pay it, you will have the fear of it being shut off.

The same goes for rent, car payment, a present for a loved one on their birthday, buying food, gas for your car, or anything that you classify as essential for your lifestyle.

Perspective plays a big role in the fears that develop right in front of your eyes. It's important to note that fears are not in you. What's in you is the reaction to the fear, the emotion that stirs inside you.

Fear is a situation for which you have no answer. It's not inside you so you have the choice to face it and do something about it. Far too often we run away from our fears, but they just follow us because we don't do anything to change the situation we're in.

If you do something about the situation, your fear will disappear. It won't be able to develop. We'll discuss how to do that later. So, for now, let's get back to the G.O.A.T. The greatest fear of all time.

What is the greatest fear of all time? Some would say heights, social anxiety, spiders, certain animals, dying, getting sick, closed places, and fear of the dark. If you have fear in one of these areas, it's most likely because of an experience that you had.

In this book, we are going to discuss the other category of fears, the everyday variety of surprises. These fears arise from unexpected situations like losing your job, a sudden illness, an accident, a change in relationship status.

I loved dogs growing up but one day, when I was around 8 years old, I was bitten by one while walking home from school. I was scared to death, it hurt bad. I was bleeding from my hand and ran all the way home. Then there was an additional fear of having to get rabies shots in my stomach with those long needles if we couldn't find the dog. This caused me to fear all dogs for several years.

After that incident, you couldn't get me near a dog without having a fight on your hands. But I overcame my fear of dogs after my parents brought a new puppy home. He was loving and playful as puppies are. My revised experience with my new dog helped rid me of my fear of dogs and the result is that I love dogs to this very day. My parents were very creative in how they made me face my fears and through that, I was able to overcome it. The solution to my unresolved situation was to have me care for an innocent loving puppy.

Your fears are borne out of similar situations and can have similar results. To overcome your greatest personal fears, you must address your unresolved situations for which you don't have an answer for and in which you've previously experienced failure. You are living each day afraid of the unknown or a repeat failure every time you are faced with this situation. And I know you don't want to live with that kind of rain cloud over your head.

If you honestly examine your life, you will find that your greatest fears often change from time to time. Why is that? It could be that you are now dealing with a new situation that scares you more or you have just run from a previous fear that remains unresolved.

When an athlete is a G.O.A.T. they win all the time. Do you want to live your life with fear

14

winning all the time and being a champion in your life? No.

You need to realize is there is no G.O.A.T. in the area of fears. There are only current situations. If you take this viewpoint, you will approach your fears differently. They won't be as overwhelming. They will no longer be fears and will become something you can manage and control instead of letting it control you.

Fear is a state of despair where there are no answers and a bad outcome cannot seemingly be changed. Fear causes mental paralysis and it impels you to stop working to make the situation better. You just wait for the other shoe to drop, so to speak.

Approach fear as a situation and seek out help for solutions and options. If nothing can stop the inevitable, then plan for the impact.   It may be a bad situation but planning for the impact will help you recover sooner.

My G.O.A.T. Statement

"Fear is not a champion in my life and will not consistently win in my situations. There is no greatest of all-time fear in my consciousness. I will always evaluate my options and if I cannot stop the bad outcome. I will prepare for its arrival and be ready to deal with it positively."

Yes

"Saying No is a denial. Saying Yes is a confession. It is owning the moment, taking responsibility, declaring I've got this, and doing something about it."

Do you have fears? Please say yes because we both know we all have them. Own your fears and attack them one by one until they are gone. When a new one rears its ugly head, attack it as well by evaluating your options, asking for help when needed, settle on an option, then execute or brace for impact.

"No, I'm not afraid" is a denial and a lie. All of us are afraid of something. The feeling may last years or but for a moment, but it's healthy and normal to be afraid. What you do with that fear is what matters. Are you going to let it manage you or are you going to manage it? This marks the difference between a relatively happy life and one filled with rollercoasters of emotion.

Get in the habit of responding Yes to everything. Crazy, right? Not at all. Look at the contrast between these two people. They are no different than you or me. And after

16

reading their experience, ask yourself who would you rather be?

One has a Yes attitude and the other has a No attitude. Think of something you have been afraid of in the past and how you handled it. Did you own it and take action or did you lie to yourself, and say, *"I got this"*, and then take no action?

If you approached your fear with a *"No, I'm not afraid"* attitude. You are lying to yourself because there is a fear there. Acknowledge it and say, *"Yes that's a scary thought but this is what I'm going to do about it"* or *"this is how I'm going to prepare for the impact of what's coming."*

When you say "No I'm not afraid", you tend to ignore the facts and stop working on the situation. You accept the current status and draw your line in the sand in front of your protection. All you're doing is waiting to see what happens. Don't do this. Fear causes mental paralysis where you feel so overwhelmed, you can't do anything to help yourself. So, you are doing what fear wants. It wants you to do nothing.

If someone was about to hit you, do you just stand there and take the blow? Or do you attempt to block the punch and then deliver one of your own. The latter is how you should approach fear. Beat its ass!

There is more fight in you to overcome the bad outcome you're expecting than you realize. What if there are no solutions? Then your strategy is to prepare and brace for impact.

Meet Mel and Norman. They are both great people. They have good friends, nice jobs, and good health.

Mel is happy the majority of the time and approaches situations from a positive standpoint. She has learned how to consistently defeat fear and use it to her advantage. She is the G.O.A.T. when it comes to fear. Fear has lost to Mel several times.

Norman has several ups and downs each month. A few weeks ago, he heard a rumor that sparked fear and now the emotions inside him are giving birth to anxiety and a depressed state of mind. He's not afraid of everything, but when something unexpected comes his way, he panics and lets the emotional tidal wave soak him with doubt, frustration, and helplessness. It also dictates his response.

Mel and Norman both heard rumors that their department was facing budget cuts and that there was a possibility a few people would be let go. How would you react to a rumor like this?

Would you say, *"Whatever, if they let me go, I'll just find something else?"* Or would you look at it as a situation you can do something about?

Rumors have now swirled around the office for three months about layoffs, how many people would be let go, and which positions were at risk. What would you have done during these three months? Would you have waited to see what would happen or prepare so you would have options no matter what happened?

Early Rumor Stage

Mel decided early on to do something to change her situation. She had no control over who would get laid off or when, so she decided to change herself. She proactively decided to make herself more valuable by getting additional training that would help her do her job better and put herself on track to be promoted.

If they were considering laying her off, she wanted to make their decision as hard as possible and put herself in a position that would make it easier to land another job if she lost this one.

Mel worked out two options and prepared for impact. This was her attitude...

"Yes, I'm afraid of losing my job so I have looked into additional training that can enhance my skills so I will be more valuable to my current employer and also more attractive in the job market if I do have to start looking.

In fact, I'm going to start looking now so I can see what my options are and that will help me be better prepared and more confident in dealing with all these rumors.

A couple of weeks later these were her thoughts... *Wow, I can't believe I'm not stressing over this. I'm getting good sleep every night; I feel great about myself and I don't care what happens because I have options now. If I left, I would miss my friends but I would be leaving on a good note and they will be good references for me as well. I truly am in a good place despite the rumors."*

Norman, on the other hand, didn't do anything to change his situation. He had a No attitude. When people asked him how he felt about the rumors, he always responded, *"I'll be ok"* or" I'm *not worried about it"*, but he was. It was evident in his attitude and irritability over almost everything. He stopped being friendly, stopped helping people as he usually does because he didn't want anyone to look better than him.

So, Norman did the No. He did nothing about his situation and ignored it. Here are some of the things he stopped doing.

- Looking for ways to make himself more valuable in his employer's eye's
- Assisting co-workers around the office when they had questions or needed help to complete an assignment
- Being the nice, friendly Norman that his colleagues loved to be around
- Being as valuable to his company as he had been before
- Looking for ways to better himself.

Norman stopped being Norman. He didn't formulate any options or prepare for impact, he just braced for it. This was his attitude...

"I'm not afraid if they fire me, I'll just pick up the pieces and move on. But I'll tell you what I'm not going to help anyone else until this is over. There's no way that I'm going to help someone look good and then they let me go.

If they do let me go, I can always find another job and I do have some savings set aside to hold me over if it takes a while to catch on somewhere. Man, I hope they don't fire me though. I would rather stay and hold onto my savings and I like this job."

A few weeks later Norman's thoughts were... *"I am so tired from tossing and turning all night. I can't stop thinking about this and I'm starting to feel sick. I just wish all of this was over so I could just go look for another job"*

Which one of these two good people is like you? Now it is true that they are at opposite ends of the spectrum, but which one is closest to the person you are?

This is something that happens to people all the time. You might have a different fear but all fears can be handled the same way. Your fear or situation can be anything. It could be health, a relationship, competition for a job, a sports scholarship, finances, or transportation.

No matter the situation how would you want to handle it? Like Mel or like Norman. Who do you want to be? Think about that for a moment.

It Is True

Today it was confirmed during a staff meeting that two people will be let go by the end of the week. Everyone in the room, including Mel and Norman looked at each other. Norman shrugged his shoulders and said to himself, *"whatever"*, then tried unsuccessfully to hide his concern while unknowingly mumbling out loud, *"I can't believe this is happening."* The rest of the staff had worried looks on their faces as well, wondering if they would be one of the two let go. Mel sat back in her chair, confident and at peace, with a relaxed calm over her face.

During the remainder of the week, Mel brushed up her resume and continued her training. She also set up some interviews to see how viable her options were. Who knows, she might get a better offer and decide to leave on her own.

The Aftermath

The day has come and the notices go out. Mel and Norman both get laid off. This is not a good day for either of them but even though they shared the same outcome, they do not share the same outcome.

How is that? To act or not to act is a better question. What happened here is that Mel had planned to do something about it two months ago and Norman didn't do anything at all. He let the chips fall where they may and boy did they fall, all over him.

The First 2 weeks After The Layoffs

The first two weeks were not that bad for either of them since they still had a week of pay coming and a nice severance payment which included unused vacation time.

But that is where the similarities ended. Mel had taken 3 interviews for jobs the week she was laid off and was offered a better position by a competitor with lots of room for growth. She would make more money and be challenged to reach even higher goals with her new company.

The additional training Mel was taking fit perfectly with the goals her new manager set out for her. Mel identified her options from the outset and it paid off when she received the news that she would no longer be working there. She wasn't lucky, she was prepared.

Norman was shocked and hurt at the news. He didn't know what to do, so he just left and went home. He didn't say goodbye to anyone. How could he? He had no plan and did not want to face anyone.

Norman received a nice severance and had 4 weeks of vacation pay coming. He reasoned that he would give himself 4 weeks to find something and use the vacation pay to fund the time spent searching for a job. Where would he start? There were no immediate prospects and his resume was not up to date.

Norman spent the next two weeks putting together his resume and trying to secure good references. Now he would begin his search.

The Two Months After

Mel loves her new job and her manager has painted a very promising career path that Mel is very excited about. She thought to herself...

"I'm so glad I didn't panic and give in to those initial feelings of fear. My plan worked out perfectly and now I'm in a much better place with more security and better pay. And since my new job started so soon, I was able to add all of my severance and vacation pay to my savings, almost doubling it. Getting laid off was one of the best things that have ever happened to me."

It took Norman five weeks to find a job. He is making about the same but it has been a very long journey and Norman has had many disappointing moments along the way. Norman is thinking...

"I wish I had started looking when I first heard those rumors. I could have found a job sooner and could have saved a lot of that money and I wouldn't have been so stressed. Now I have a

new job that is ok, but it's not exactly what I wanted. I'm going to keep looking and hopefully, I'll find something I like down the road."

What outcome would you want for yourself? Whether its health, money, a relationship, an issue on your job, competing in sports, or in the classroom, we all have challenges. The outcome you experience is wholly dependent on what you do about it and when.

Are you going to stand there and fight or stand there and get hit?

If your reaction time in boxing is slow, you are going to get hit over and over again. If your reaction time to fear is slow, you are going to be overwhelmed with emotion, doubt, thoughts of failure, stress, and more, over and over again.

Do you see the pattern? Say Yes, admit the fear is there, then do something about the situation and do it right now.

Your reaction time is key. Mel reacted almost immediately and is reaping the benefits thereof because she didn't wait to do something about her fear of being laid off. She eliminated fear and replaced it with hope and a solid plan.

Every action causes a reaction as the saying goes in science. Mel took action two months ago when she first heard the rumors. The reaction was a landing a new job immediately after being told she was let go and doubling her savings because she didn't have a gap in income.

Norman did not act and there was no reaction to his favor in this situation until he acted two months after he heard the rumors. Once he acted it took five additional weeks to get a job and he burned through a lot of the money he could have saved. Norman also stressed the whole time and didn't end up where he wanted to be.

Who are you going to be? Mel or Norman?

My Yes Statement

"I'll never lie to myself and say I don't fear anything. Yes, I am afraid sometimes but I fight through it. I manage fear by seeking help, encouragement, and advice so I can have options. Then I execute. If there is no solution, I accept the situation for what it is and plan for how to deal with the implications when they come. I'll never run and I fight the hardest when I am afraid. So, bring it on!"

Inspire

"You can't do anything without being inspired.
We are inspired every day either to victory or
defeat. Where there is little Hope,
Fear inspires us to defeat"

What inspires and motivates you to action? Money, ambition, people, family, fame, material possessions, your inner drive? When you are inspired you are encouraged to start something or continue something even when it appears all is lost, chances are slim, and all odds are against you.

When you think about inspiration, you think of positive outcomes. You're thinking of reaching goals or achieving victory over someone or something. The person or thing that inspires you will influence you, arouse a desire or feeling in you, it will impel you to act and produce something.

Think about this for a moment... you can be inspired to produce something positive, influenced to do something great, aroused to develop awesome ideas, and impelled to bring them to fruition, however, this can also go the other way.

28

Why do I say that? When you examine your fears, you'll realize that if left unchecked, fears inspire you too. They influence you to lose hope and quit. They arouse feelings of desperation. Fear produces doubt and impels you to do nothing and wait for the bad thing to happen or makes you run away to avoid the situation.

Fear inspires defeat. So, it's important to confront your fears and not run away from them. Treat your fears as what they are, situations. A situation can be resolved or prepared for. The only way to resolve the emotions brought on by fear is to deal with the situations causing them.

Feelings of fear go away when the situation changes.

Say you haven't heard from your young adult child in 3 days. Up to this point, you talk to him every day, but now he is not answering his phone or emails.

You start to worry and you begin to fear that something is wrong. Is he hurt? Did something tragic happen? Where is he? Did he have an accident and the hospital doesn't know how to contact you?

So, what do you do now? As your fear grows with each minute, you start calling hospitals and maybe even the police to see if something bad has happened. Fear inspired your feelings and actions. Fear influenced you to do things, impelled you to act, aroused feelings, and produced sadness.

But wait, he calls and he is fine, safe, and healthy. He apologizes for not calling you back and explains that he was upset that he broke up with his girlfriend and he got caught up in his feelings and didn't want to talk to or be around anyone.

Where is your fear now? It's gone in the blink of an eye because the situation has changed. Your son isn't in the danger you imagined, but he is hurt emotionally. So now you go into loving parent mode and talk him through it. You aren't sad anymore. You're very happy because your son is alright and the fear that beat you down earlier is nowhere in sight.

What made the fear go away? The fear went away because the situation has changed.

Be inspired to not give up. You don't have to constantly live in the same situation, but if it can't be changed, then make a change in you. Don't ever let both you and the situation stay the same. That's doing nothing and that's how fear wins.

To be fair, some situations like health, finances, and relationships might not be able to be changed. But you can still do something about those situations. You can change you.

You can seek help for health issues and plan for how to adjust your life to accommodate your illness. This is the preparation part for instances where you have no control. It does make it better and manageable to a certain degree. You face it and fight.

Finances can be confronted in several different ways. Maybe you don't need more money, you just need to manage it better. If more money is needed seek out help from friends, family, and charitable organizations. Look for government programs designed to assist folks that are in your situation.

Problems in a relationship tend to be more complicated and generate fears from several angles. But as stated before, you address the situation, not how you are feeling.

The fears people experience in relationships share the common thread of what will happen if you honestly share how you feel about something or share something very private.

No matter the form of the relationship, we maintain a fear of how people see and judge us. This kind of fear inspires us to lie and be

31

dishonest in the relationship. It affects what we say and do. We are afraid of how the other person will react. Will they get mad? Will they think of me differently? Will my honesty harm our relationship?

We give in to fear and say yes when we want to say no. Thus, we agree to something we don't want. While it is true that some things are best left unsaid and you can't tell everyone everything, you do need to cultivate genuine relationships with your spouse, siblings, parent, child, and close friends where you can be yourself and express yourself honestly without judgment and repercussions.

You must be able to let people close to you know when something they said hurt you and you need to feel free to go to them with private things. If you openly share your feelings and thoughts you are more likely not to be asked or pressured to do things that you do not want to do. You will also find out who respects your feelings. It forces honesty in the relationship.

How can you change yourself to cultivate a more genuine relationship? Well, whether you are sharing bad news, responding to bad news, or sharing something intimate or honest about yourself, be kind, humble, and gracious. Identify your part in the situation and try to keep your emotions on an even keel.

Keep in mind how you would like to receive the message you are about to deliver. If you are struggling to share in honesty, find someone to go with you to help deliver the message.

Lastly, don't go into the conversation with expectations of how the person should respond. Keep an open mind and examine your expectations against the reality of what that person is capable of handling.

You overcome fear in relationships by being brave, courageous, and saying what needs to be said in the right way, in love. Inspire the other person in the conversation to be accepting, gracious, and appreciative of your honesty and respect for them by how you deliver the news.

You can use all of your fears to inspire you to make changes in yourself that will make the situation better and make you a better person. Keep the *"I'm never going to let this happen again"* and *"I'm going to make this better"* mentality in your spirit. You've said that before, right? After something has gone wrong and you survived it?

That's your inspiration right there. You can make changes in yourself and what's in your control to prevent the situation from happening again or put something in place as a buffer to distance yourself from the impact.

Nothing always works perfectly, but you can change things and prepare yourself so that you have far less to deal with if a bad outcome is on its way.

The calm before the storm is a very popular term. I've used it myself at times. People say this when they expect something bad to happen and fear something horrible that they have no control over will soon take place.

Remember Mel and Norman? They also have spoken the words, *"This is the calm before the storm."* The difference is that while Norman waits on the storm, Mel works to extend the calm. Her attitude is I want the calm INSTEAD of the storm.

Don't let fear inspire you to a defeated ego, defeated goals, defeated feelings of despair, or to allow people to hurt and not respect you. Let fear inspire you to be better, grow, build, anticipate, and improve your life in the best way possible.

Ask yourself... What inspires or encourages me to continue when it seems all is lost, my chances are slim, and all odds are against me? Find that and you will be well on your way to conquering fear.

My Inspire Statement

"Fear will never inspire me to fail. I will never allow fear to defeat me. I will do something about the situation that is causing the fear. If I can't change the situation, I will change me."

Fight

*"You never know how strong you are until
being strong is the only choice you have.
Don't stop fighting until the fight is over."*

Fear will come at you in two ways. It either pushes you forward so you move on to something else before it can be resolved or it holds you back to keep you from progressing to something you need to do. Whichever way fear pushes or pulls you; you have to immediately go HARD in the opposite direction.

What makes this hard to do sometimes is another component of fear, worrying. Worry fuels fear. It's like topping off your car with gas so you can drive around all day on a full tank. Worry fuels the emotions caused by fear and keeps them going all day and all night.

To fight against fear, you have to learn how to stop worrying and turn yourself into a problem solver. Remember the suggestion earlier that sometimes it's you that has to change?

Examine how you've handled things in the past with the fears you are still dealing with. Fear will push you toward the path of least resistance. We're talking about the initial steps you usually took in dealing with that fear, not the initial thoughts.

The initial thoughts may have had all the good intentions in the world and they may have been brave and well thought out, but you took the easiest and most comfortable way which is sometimes to simply do nothing. This is a normal occurrence with recurring fears.

What can you do to change the cycle? Change yourself and be stronger, braver. You'll have to fight yourself to not take the easiest or shortest path to relief. You have to take the right path. Keep in mind that fear pushes you away from what you should be doing. So, do what you know needs to be done. Do the right thing here.

Take the case of Mel and Norman. Mel became a problem solver for a problem that didn't yet exist. She reduced or mitigated risk by doing contingency planning. Large corporations and governments keep contingency plans in place, so if a certain event happens, they know exactly what to do to protect themselves and survive it.

I used to work for a mining company that produced and sold a copper. When the stock market crashed in 2008, the price of copper dropped as well. They had contingency plans in place based on how far the price of copper fell. At a certain price, they would do layoffs or slow production. If it fell further, they would shut down a mine. These triggers were in place so they could control the fate of the company and keep it profitable. Every time copper hit a certain price; they executed the plan.

Governments have several contingency plans based on the stock market levels, global trade, what other countries do, and war. If and when certain events take place, triggers, they execute the plan to protect the country.

Mel had a contingency plan in place. She planned to make herself more valuable in case she got laid off. She improved her skillset, updated her resume, and took a few interviews with companies for practice to get a feel for her value in the workplace.

The goal was to minimize the gap in employment so she would not have to dip into her savings. So, if she did get laid off, trigger, she would start the real interviewing and be well ahead of the game.

When Mel received the official news that she would be laid off, trigger, she immediately contacted the company that had shown the most interest and she got the job.

Norman didn't have a contingency plan. It was easier to do nothing and so that's what he did. There was no plan or preparation. His initial steps contrasted Mel's in every way. Mel put a lot of effort into her plan and she executed it perfectly and on time.

She took classes after work, got professional help in updating her resume, and started spending more time helping others with their assignments so she would be more valuable to her employers. In the end, it didn't matter because she was still laid off, but it did pay off in that she got something much, much better. A new job and a doubling of her savings.

Looking back, if that were you, would you have rather kept the old job or received the outcome that Mel had? She ended up much better off than if she hadn't got laid off. And that will be the topic of another book.

Norman had no contingency so he wasn't prepared for the event that should have served as a trigger for him. The layoff was a trigger for Mel and she acted on it. Norman had nothing and lost even more.

To beat fear, you have to change your mindset, the set of rules by which you operate. Fear tries to dictate those rules to you and have you follow them every time it comes along. Make your own rules and fight back.

Where will that fight take you? It will take you to some very uncomfortable places. Places that you may have never let yourself go before.

One of the first stops is the urge to settle for less. Why stop when you are almost there and you can have more? It might seem like there is no progress but there is. Don't settle for good enough and give up. *"I gave it a good shot"* isn't always the best you could have done. There is still room to do better.

Feelings of criticism, failure, and rejection can be enough to make you quit or not even try. But don't let this hold you back. Why care about what others think when it's you and your loved ones that have to live with the situation and the outcomes? Fight these feelings and do what you need to do, say what you need to say.

Your family and your well-being are far more important than someone's opinion. Don't give in to the fear of what other people think when you have an opportunity to make a change and do better.

Saying yes when you mean no, not asking questions, and not asking for help are devastating blows you should not inflict upon yourself as you seek solutions in the fight against fear.

First, you don't get the help you need, and then comes the feeling of shame which lowers your self-esteem even more. If you keep doing this, you'll be so ashamed of yourself that you'll never ask for help and no one will be able to help you fight.

You also have to fight against numbing your pain through food, alcohol, technology, and being so excessively busy that you don't think about your problem. However, your problem will quietly wait until you're finished ignoring it until it can resume its conflict with you. Overindulging in these activities does nothing to resolve your fears but could lead to other serious problems you'll have to deal with.

Fear makes you procrastinate and causes you to struggle with making decisions. *"I don't know what to do."* Well, ask for help, pray, seek out a trusted friend or family member you can talk to. You don't have to fight on your own. Form a team and together you can win.

Reach out to people who have successfully overcome the same situation or fear that you are dealing with. The most important thing is to not wait to reach out. Your best decision is not what you do to solve the problem. Your best decision will be how soon you ask for help.

Other things you need to fight against are trying to control everything around you. You can only control you. Focus on what you can change in you that will make a difference in your situation.

Above all do not shut down and not let your voice be heard. If you can't handle this and need help, ask for it. If people are hurting you, then tell then. And don't be afraid to ask for what you want, how you want to be treated.

If you don't fight for the things above, fear will be a regular part of your life. You'll also risk becoming physically sick due to the worry and anxiety you feel. These emotions cause a stress response that your body cannot handle.

Fear holds you back from progressing into the individual, friend, and family you are destined to be. Don't let fear beat you. Make changes and it will go away.

My Fight Statement

"I will fight fear to the death; until it dies. I will ask for help when needed. My "yes" will mean yes, and my "no" will mean no. I will let people know when they are hurting me and I will not fight alone."

Lose

"You are not defeated when you lose. You are defeated when you quit. Let's work on losing because you have to learn how to lose, to win."

You have to learn how to lose, to win against fear. Sounds crazy, right? Well, for one, you have to stop trying to be perfect and you can never quit. Stop worrying about not being good enough. Stop looking for advice in the wrong places from inexperienced and negative people. Above all, stop putting yourself down. You have to lose these things. You also have to forget.

When you lose something, you don't have access to it anymore and it can't influence your life for good or bad. You may find it again, but while it's lost, it's effect or value is of no use and has no power over you. Let's first talk about losses and then things you have to lose.

If you dwell on your losses, your mindset changes and you lose confidence. You can't perform and handle things in the way you're capable of because you think it will happen again, so why try. If you lose something that has good value then by all means see if there is a way to recover it. But if that thing brings bad value to your life, leave it behind. Remember the lesson there, but more forward and realize that you can do better next time. You aren't stuck where you have to get the same result every time, but to get a different result you have to do something differently.

In sports, a skilled player can have a bad play, but if they can't forget that last play and move on to the next one, their play diminishes and gets worse. They lose confidence and become inconsistent, unable to bounce back and make plays when they are needed.

The game of basketball is a great example of this. Let's look at two basketball players who are teammates, Chris and Derek. A great player, Chris, and an average player, Derek, both miss their first seven shots. There was a particular fan who was a regular at all of the games that proceeded to boo and call both Chris and Derek names. He was letting them have it for missing all those shots. Derek starts thinking I better stop shooting and just pass and play defense. He quits shooting.

Chris is thinking I know the next one is going in. He never quit shooting. Derek did and ended up being of no value to the team when they needed him. The team had gotten behind by 12 points. Chris kept on shooting even

45

though he was having an off night. Then he finally started making shots again.

He now has made 5 shots in a row and the team is within 2 points of the lead. Derek is also on that team but he has given in to his fear of missing and has quit shooting. He is playing well but he is passing up wide-open shots. This causes the other team to double-team Chris and he is unable to get a good shot at the basket, but he is looking to shot.

Derek was on the court during a crucial time in the game with the team coming back from a large deficit and having a chance to take the lead. He is now proving to be of less value to himself and the team and the other team is leaving him wide open, knowing he won't shoot.

There are 30 seconds left in the game and they are down by 1 point. The ball gets around to Chris and he shoots but misses, his other teammate Kurt gets the rebound and draws a foul. He makes both free throws and they take the lead by 1. The other team comes down and after a few good passes make another basket and are now up by 1 point once again.

Derek takes the ball out and passes to Chris with 14 seconds left in the game. Chris dribbles up and passes to Kurt. He is trapped and the only outlet is to Derek who is wide open. Kurt passes to Derek who starts to dribble. Derek is so consumed by his fear of missing that it becomes bigger than his opportunity to win. He was "this" close to overcoming his fear. All he had to do was take another shot.

Hell, Derek didn't even want the ball. He quit before he had a chance to quit. With his heart racing and fear rising, Derek looked to see who he could pass the ball to so they could take the shot. He passed to Chris, who somehow got open and although missing his last attempt, he shot again and made it.

Overall, the team won the game, but Derek's reluctance to shot almost caused them to lose. He was released from the team a few weeks later because he lost all his confidence and couldn't be counted on to help the team in pressure situations. No other team signed him either, citing his poor play under pressure and not being dependable.

Derek could have taken that shot and even if missed, another teammate could have gotten the rebound. Players aren't expected to make every shot and certainly not to make all of their last-second shots, but they are expected to shot under pressure.

Chris, on the other hand, was dependable, consistent, and looked for opportunities to win amid pressure and missed opportunities. He beat his opponent because he did not quit. Chris ended up becoming the MVP of the tournament and proved once again that you cannot be defeated if you do not quit.

A great fighter in the fight against fears is dependable, consistent, and never quits on themselves or the people depending on them.

If you look at consistency here, it's not the number of shots you make that's important, it's the fact that you can be counted on to take another one if the previous ones were not successful. Be consistent by continuing to fight your fears. Don't stop because you have a setback and missed success. Keep "shooting" until you are successful like Chris was.

Also, people are more apt to help you if they see you trying. This is the help that you don't expect but desperately need.

Sports are very much a mental game and so is going up against your fears. You have to forget that battle you lost the last time and move forward with your fight. Before that last shot, Chris received some unexpected support. The fan that had relentlessly booed and heckled him now saw Chris's strength and determination. He started to cheer and as Chris came up the court, he yelled out, *"you've got this Chris. Get your shot."* This gave Chris the added determination he needed to get open for that last shot.

Sometimes help comes from unexpected places and gives us what we need to take that last shot at success. Don't get distracted by your fear and only see or hear what your fear is telling you. Take a breath and take in your surroundings. There could be something or someone very close trying to encourage you.

So far, we've talked about losing in terms of you trying to win against an opponent. Now let's examine another aspect of losing. This involves things you need to let go of to win.

When you lose an object or relationship you can't always get it back. It could be gone forever. You can wish you had it all you want but it's just not going to be available to you. You must lose these things on purpose. This is how you need to treat the people and things that are holding you back from overcoming your fears. You should especially do this with your memories. Lose them and continue your fight.

If you want to be broke, hang around broke people. You pick up the habits of the people around you, so hang out with people that will make you better. Get rid of people that breed negativity and surround yourself with people that don't add to your problem. Your circle should give you the hope of something better.

We also harbor fears because we think we're not good enough. Remember Derek the basketball player, who missed as many shots as Chris? Derek didn't take another shot in that game because he gave in to his fear. And although being one of the top players in the world, Derek believed he was not good enough.

The fear of losing a relationship, that we'll be abandoned, that we'll be rejected are all tied to believing we're not good enough. This keeps you from speaking the truth about how you feel when you are hurt. It makes you stop trying. It makes you quit. We fear intimacy for the very same reason. Even the fear of success is based on the worry that we're not good enough to achieve or sustain it, and we expect the bad result instead of success.

One last thing... Your fight with fear is a war, made up of several battles. If you do it right, you will win by losing. You are at war and you may have many battles with your fears before you win your war against them. If you lose a battle, don't quit. Go to battle again by losing your memory of the loss. Be like Chris and take another shot at it. Don't ever quit. Strive to change the situation and if you can't, make the change in you and keep it pushing.

My Lose Statement

"I will lose everything that inspires me to quit. I am willing to learn how to lose to understand what it takes to win. I will take every setback and learn from them. I will seek out other people who have conquered the same fears I have and learn from the lessons they have learned."

Win

"You are more than capable of winning. Just don't get caught up in how long it might take."

How do you win against fear? By consistently fighting to make your situations better. Fight to not quit. Remember that fear is the result of a situation your facing. So, focus on changing the situation or yourself and you will defeat fear.

You will always have fears, but when you get to a place where you are no longer driven by them, something special happens. You become rich. You are in touch with your value. You feel powerful. Alive. Worthy.

Your anxiety lessens and potential increases, which means the chances of you improving the quality of your life increases as well as things fall into place. You become very potent and start to be mentally aware of others in trouble and you are available and can help them through their struggles.

When you're going to take on an adversary, you prepare yourself. You train, develop a battle plan, and arm yourself. Do this in your battle against your fear.

We've all heard the old saying, "Practice makes perfect." If you treat your losses as practice, you will become a perfect opponent for fear.

If you want to be great at something it looks like this... practice, practice, practice, gaining all the skills and information you need to succeed, then you practice some more. You continue to apply the lessons learned in previous battles and work on getting better and better. Over time, you improve until you reach a level where you consistently beat your opponent.

If you want to be great relative to your fear, be willing to... lose, lose, lose, apply the lessons learned in those losses, and work on getting better at handling it. Each time see if you can change something in the situation or change something in you. Then try again.

Be in the moment. Fear of failure and other fears are all based on the future. Far too many times, we get caught up worrying about what might happen in the future instead of making something happen now. You have to think about the moment you are in and forget about past mistakes and failures to keep fighting and win this thing.

Do something right now in your situation that will positively affect your future. This is how you beat your fears and pursue your dreams. Forget about what might happen later. As Nike says, Just Do It, now, at this moment. When you find yourself thinking about the past or future, bring yourself back into the moment and focus on what you're doing right now.

Start by taking small steps. Conquering fear and pursuing a new life free of it can be overwhelming, and intimidating. So, start small. Just take one tiny baby step. Something you know you can do. Something you're sure to succeed at. Then allow yourself to feel good about it and take another small baby step. Keep doing this, and soon you'll have conquered one of your fears.

Celebrate every success! Every single thing you do right, celebrate it. Even the smallest thing. And use this feeling of success, of victory, to propel yourself forward and take the next step. Build upon each success and use it as a stepping stone to the next victory.

To consistently win, you will have to prepare mentally, physically, and spiritually. Mental preparation requires a continuous cycle of setting the right expectations and keeping the right perspective.

Your mental preparation for victory may develop from within or it may come with help from a coach or counselor. When my son was in high school, I coached the basketball team in a rec league he and his friends were going to play on.

We had nine players; most were from his football team. Of the nine, only 4 were really good shooters and I know from experience that when a player that isn't a good shooter starts missing shots, they get nervous and start making mistakes. So, I instituted a rule for the whole team that if you are open and have a good shot at the basket, take the shot.

I also told them I didn't care if they missed, just keep shooting. Why did I do this? There were two reasons.

1. I didn't want the opponent to double-team any of our players. If I know a player isn't going to shoot, I won't have my players guard him. I'll have them help out on a better player who will shoot. This gives the defense the advantage and puts the offense at a disadvantage. I taught them to pass, rebound, play defense, and always take a good shot.

   If one of our guys that didn't shoot as well took a shot, we still stood a good chance to get the rebound if he missed. It didn't matter if he made the shot or not, we just needed him to keep shooting. This allowed us to keep their defense spread out and we would just out-hustle them for the rebound if there was a miss.

2. I wanted all of my players to be confident every minute they were in the game. As the coach, me telling them I didn't care if they missed, erased any fear they might have of missing a shot. If they missed, it didn't matter to me and so it didn't matter to them as long as it was a good shot. This gave them the confidence to continue shooting no matter how many shots they missed. This same confidence allowed them to play all other aspects of the game without fear.

How did this strategy pay off? It kept the players engaged and made all of them feel important to the team. Shooting is the main thing by which players are judged, so by removing the importance of accuracy, there was no pressure to make shots, only to take them. It also killed any trash talking between my players about anyone missing. It made them more encouraging to one another.

There were several instances during the season where our star players purposely passed up good shots to create even better ones for our lessor players. And if they made the shot, our boys on the court would cheer louder than the fans watching them. We were truly a team in the purest sense.

All of my players were instructed to not be afraid to shoot. We placed their focus on passing, defense, and getting rebounds. Can you imagine how Derek might have responded differently in that game with Chris if he had this same mentality, to keep shooting if it is a good shot?

This concept paid off for us in a game where at halftime we were losing 15 – 9. That's right, it was a very low scoring game. We were averaging around 50 points a game and our low score at halftime wasn't the result of the other team playing great defense. It was bad shooting on our part, not bad shots. We took good shots, they just weren't going in.

Usually, at halftime, your team has a chance to take practice shots at the new basket, but I wouldn't let them. Instead, I made them sit and spoke to them. They assumed I would be mad and yell at them but I didn't. I asked what they thought was wrong. Some said we were rushing our shots, we need to get more rebounds, we need to focus better, etc.

I looked at each one of them and told them that they played a great first half and that they did everything I asked of them. They looked at me like I was crazy because they knew the score should have been much higher. Some said, *"look at the score," "we were terrible," "we missed way too many shots."*

They felt dejected and had the looks on their faces to match. We were the best team in the league and were undefeated. Would this turn out to be our first loss of the season? Come on now, you know the answer to that.

I explained that up to this point they played a great game because they took good shots and they didn't stop shooting even though they kept missing. The strategy for the second half, was the same as the first, keep shooting and don't change a thing. The only way we would lose was if we stopped shooting.

I wanted them to see what I saw, a great team that experienced some unlucky bounces. I told the team I didn't care if they missed every shot for the rest of the game, just keep shooting. This was key and it freed their minds of any worry, doubt, or fear that had built up from their performance in the first half of taking another shot. It helped them forget all about those missed shots.

They went back on the court with a renewed confidence realizing that after playing their worst half of the season, they were only down by 6 points. They also realized if they only made one 3-pointer, they would have cut the lead in half. Newborn confidence is a beautiful thing.

As a coach, I helped them visualize their performance and position from a different perspective and it changed the outcome of the game. They went back out there and battled. They kept focused on passing, defense, and rebounds. They also remembered our mantra to keep taking good shots.

At half-time, we were behind 15 – 9. We then outscored them by 19 points in the second half and won the game 37 – 24. It was our lowest scoring game, but it was our greatest victory. We held them to only 9 points in the second half and went on to have an undefeated season for the second year in a row.

Our team would routinely have the game won by halftime most of the time. Yes, victory usually came early in our contests, but in this particular game, it did not. It took a little longer than expected. When victory in your life takes longer than you expect, don't quit, just keep on shooting.

In the battle against your fears, you may miss a lot of good shots at defeating your fears. You may have done everything right and still did not get the results you were expecting, but that doesn't mean you never will. Just keep taking those good shots.

There are three types of preparation you must incorporate into your life to win. You must prepare mentally, physically, and spiritually. Mental preparation requires a continuous cycle of setting the right expectations and keeping the right perspective. A coach or counselor can help you see outside the box and help you reevaluate your position from time to time to ensure you are seeing things clearly.

Physical preparation involves taking care of your body. We're going to keep this simple and straight to the point. You need to get enough sleep and maintain a regular sleep pattern. This ensures your body and mind are getting enough rest and it keeps you on a regular eating pattern as well.

Fear and anxiety cause you to lose sleep and your appetite which causes even more stress to your body. Maintaining regularity in these two areas will do wonders for keeping your stress at minimum levels. There are many natural sleep aids designed to help you relax. You can find these at your local health food stores.

You also need to eat healthily. Stay away from processed and fast food. Drink plenty of water and eat vegetables and fruit.

This final form of preparation involves your spirituality. It's important to know that you are not alone and that fear is not from God. There may be times when you feel alone or there is no one to talk to or ask questions of. God is always there for guidance, help, and intervention whenever you need it through prayer. Pray and seek Him for guidance and direction. You are never alone when God is in your life.

Think about the victories won by Mel, Chris, by my basketball team, and the victories you've won in the past. You'll note that victory always comes to those who do not quit, but it may come at different times. Sometimes it may come immediately or early in the game. It can come at the end or it may come after going into a few overtimes.

You will win your fight against fear by following this simple formula...

• Fear is a situation. I must change the situation or I must change myself.

• I will take immediate action against the situations causing my fears. I will not hesitate to react.

- I will not stop taking good shots at defeating fear. I will never quit shooting.

- I will not expect victory at a certain time, but I will expect victory.

- I will prepare mentally, physically, and spiritually for every battle against fear.

Now that you know, what are you waiting for?

Start fighting again!

Take another shot!

And...

Expect Victory!!!

My Win Statement

"I expect victory over my fears not after a certain amount of time. I just expect it. I will continue to take good shots at overcoming fear and if I don't get the result I want, I won't quit. I may lose a battle, but I refuse to lose the war against fear."

From the Author... Thank you for taking this journey with me. If you have enjoyed this book, please go to Amazon and write your honest review. I would love your feedback on how you or someone you love were helped in your fight against fear.

The Power Statements

My G.O.A.T. Statement

"Fear is not a champion in my life and will not consistently win in my situations. There is no greatest of all-time fear in my consciousness. I will always evaluate my options and if I cannot stop the bad outcome. I will prepare for its arrival and be ready to deal with it positively."

My Yes Statement

"I'll never lie to myself and say I don't fear anything. Yes, I am afraid sometimes but I fight through it. I manage fear by seeking help, encouragement, and advice so I can have options. Then I execute. If there is no solution, I accept the situation for what it is and plan for how to deal with the implications when they come. I'll never run and I fight the hardest when I am afraid. So, bring it on!"

My Inspire Statement

"Fear will never inspire me to fail. I will never allow fear to defeat me. I will do something about the situation that is causing the fear. If I can't change the situation, I will change me. I control how long fear resides in my life."

My Fight Statement

"I will fight fear to the death; until it dies. I will ask for help when needed. My "yes" will mean yes, and my "no" will mean no. I will let people know when they are harming me and I will not fight alone.

My Lose Statement

"I will lose everything that inspires me to quit. I am willing to learn how to lose to understand what it takes to win. I will take every setback and learn from them. I will seek out other people who have conquered the same fears I have and learn from the lessons they have learned."

My Win Statement

"I expect victory over my fears not after a certain amount of time. I just expect it. I will continue to take good shots at overcoming fear and if I don't get the result I want, I won't quit. I may lose a battle, but I refuse to lose the war against fear."

What Is Your Statement?

???

Appendix

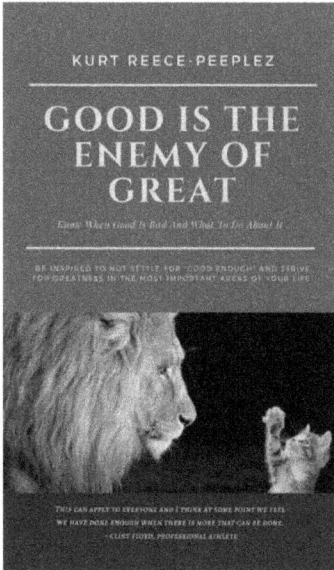

In this book, Kurt Reece-Peeplez draws on his experience as a business owner, business coach, and youth sports coach to deliver an in-depth examination of what it takes to be great and how to get there.

This easy read will inspire you to not settle for "good enough" and strive for greatness in the most important areas of your life. This book is for everyone who wants to achieve more and reach new heights.

Are you starting to follow that Good is not Good when it comes to reaching your full potential? Good can be bad if it keeps you from accomplishing something better. Many times we allow good results to stop us from achieving something greater. If this is a regular occurrence in your life, Good is your Enemy.

Read this and learn how to achieve greatness in all aspects of your life.

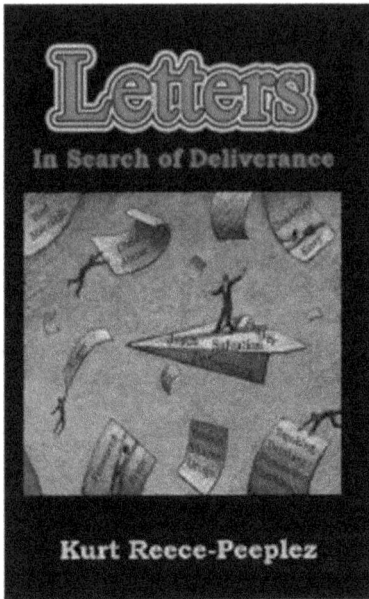

It's a fact that we all need deliverance from something. No one is on the same level as God and this is what it is all about. We are to be Holy as He is Holy, but we are imperfect. Many things can hinder spiritual growth. Most of those hindrances are hidden. They can be little things, such as the 101 in the list you've read. The point is to look at ourselves in the mirror. Look for things we may have overlooked in the past that are slowing us down spiritually in the present. We need to be delivered from them to maintain our spiritual momentum and strength.

In the book, Letters In Search of Deliverance, Author Kurt Reece-Peeplez helps us understand that we are like letters who are delivered to various places determined by how we are addressed. If it has the correct address, a letter will be delivered to the intended destination. If it has the wrong address, the letter will be delivered to the wrong place. If there is no return address, the letter may get lost or destroyed. The way you address your situations determines how successful your deliverance from them will be.

Read this book and you will:

- Find the energy to grow Spiritually Stronger

- Get the Spiritual Deliverance you are seeking.

- Determine where you are Spiritually.

- Feed your Spirit more than you Feed your Flesh.

- Obtain a complete Deliverance.

- Strengthen your Spiritual Foundation.

- Maintain your delivered state by looking to Jesus

"It all boils down to how you address your situations." Filled with several scriptural references and two simple exercises, this book helps you develop a personal plan for deliverance that works.

Notes

Notes

Notes

www.ingramcontent.com/pod-product-compliance
Lightning Source LLC
LaVergne TN
LVHW091232080426
835509LV00009B/1248